Led by the Word

Twanja Windley

PublishAmerica
Baltimore

© 2008 by Twanja Windley.
All rights reserved. No part of this book may be reproduced, stored in a retrieval system or transmitted in any form or by any means without the prior written permission of the publishers, except by a reviewer who may quote brief passages in a review to be printed in a newspaper, magazine or journal.

First printing

PublishAmerica has allowed this work to remain exactly as the author intended, verbatim, without editorial input.

ISBN: 1-60610-323-7
PUBLISHED BY PUBLISHAMERICA, LLLP
www.publishamerica.com
Baltimore

Printed in the United States of America

DEDICATION

Throughout my life God has sent some amazing people to help direct my path. I want to dedicate this book to them and tell the world how amazing these people have been to me.

- Robert Crenshaw, a wonderful MCJROTC instructor, encourages and follows me. He has traveled countless miles to see me cross stages of many accomplishments. He's dedicated and a blessing; and above all I thank God for him.
- Donald Yates, a wonderful Professor and Advisor, taught me that no matter what you do it's all about your ending. He once told me, "It's not how you start, its how you finish."
- Ms. Darneta Jones through her prayers, I've made a big difference in my life and in the lives of others. I thank her so much for believing in me.
- Dr. John Hymes my History professor at Horry-Georgetown Tech. He taught me how to write my first history paper. At nights I would cry because I didn't know what to do. He would track me down across campus daily, just to get me where I needed to be. Thank you for caring so much. I could have quit, but his unyielding desire to help me was my motivation.
- Dr. Murphy is very special to me. He reminds me of myself. He's very honest and speaks the truth. He holds no punches and gives it to me straight. He encouraged me to pursue writing this book and after knowing he approved of it, I was ready to take it to another level. I often seek advice from him and value his opinion and friendship.

- Dr. U a kind and warm hearted professor. I recall sharing some things with him after having surgery; He showed great concern and I will always remember that.
- Mr. Karns a great listener and a great professor as well. He's dedicated to helping his students maximize their potential. I thank him for his help and for listening to me as I share my stories.
- Pastor James White & First Lady White I built a great foundation at New Life Church and I will never forget that. Pastor White has always amazed me, and I prayed to be as good as he. Every Sunday I would ask God to show me how Pastor became so good, and God did. Once I became intimate with Him, all of the answers came.
- Apostle Ron Carpenter is one powerful man. I followed his ministry via television and then decided to visit his church. I realized that my faith in God is on the same level as his. He has encouraged me and like never before. I want to thank him for his deliverance of God's words. He has inspired me so much that I decided to be a part of Redemption World Outreach Church.
- Mr. Omar Tyree I thank God for allowing me to have such a wonderful mentor. I appreciate every email, phone call, and words of encouragement. I aspire to be as great as he is in my writing. He is an inspiration to me and I value his opinion and judgment. I admire him and want to let everyone know of his kindness and how instrumental he has been to my success. I know my Father is very pleased; and great things are in store for the both of us. I will continue to pray as God take his writing to the next level.

These people have gone above and beyond for me as I aim to do God's Will and I want to give thanks to them for being obedient to God. They have set quite an example for me. God has placed them in my life to help nurture and steer me in the right direction. I wanted to make sure that I acknowledge them for what they've done. These are not just teachers they are a reflection of my father in different aspects. It was these teachers that helped me to face life's obstacles and challenges. They've been a blessing to me. I thank God for allowing them to nurture me. It really does make a difference. I'm believing that as people read this they will be inspired by God's people and join us in this battle.

ACKNOWLEDGMENTS

First of all, I would like to give thanks first and foremost to God, whose lead me to write this book. Lord you made all of this possible. You lead me in my spirit and guided me through my words and to you father I say, "Thank You." Thank you for your blessings, for all of the support that you've given me, and for guiding me through the storm. Thank you for giving me the courage to write this book and most importantly the ideas to put in here, without you Lord where would I be.

When God gave me the inspiration to start writing a book, I didn't know where to begin. I always look down on myself and I felt as if I couldn't do it. With hard work and prayer God made it all possible. I began to be humble and obedient, and listened closely to what God was telling me. It takes a lot for a person to know when God is speaking to them. Pastor White taught us that we have to be sensitive to hear the voice of God. One thing that I've learned is when we pray and ask God for things we have to be obedient, humble, and patient. You have to know when God is speaking to you and move when God tells you to move. I also took the initiative to ask questions. I started communicating with Mr. Omar Tyree and he gave me that push that I needed and from there I began my journey. I honestly look up to him. He really inspires me and I value his opinion. He took time out to help me get where I needed to be. I am truly thankful.

I didn't tell many people about my work because I didn't want any setbacks, just encouragement. We all know that Satan uses people to set up stumbling blocks in our path. I kept my work between my Master, a few friends, and myself. Here it is "**Led by the Word**," and we all know that the Word is God.

TABLE OF CONTENTS

Introduction	11
In the Beginning	13
Understanding	19
Holding On	22
Making Sacrifices	25
Persevering	33
Trusting In God	37
Insight	44
God's Angel	58
Discernment	67
Because of You	72
Be Who You Are	79
Life's Struggles	93
About the Author	117

INTRODUCTION

Led by the Word is a book that God birthed into my spirit. God is allowing me to share testimonies about my life's struggles through my poetry. He has made this possible so that His words could be poured into the Earth. His goal is to touch the lives of the unsaved so that they can see that no matter what they go through they can come to Him. All they have to do is open up their hearts and tell Him yes. I am happy to be a part of this. He is allowing me to share my struggles, tell how He has provided for me, and convey when I first accepted God into my life and how Satan made me think that I wasn't good enough to serve God. It's a truly deep, yet simple story. You don't want to miss out on this word. I share some very rough times and show that if you persevere and have faith in God, it will all work out.

Through my experiences I want to reach out and let the world know that all things work together for good to them that love God, so keep your trust in Him. I wasn't always as strong as I am spiritually and I lost a lot during my childhood, but through it all I remembered that He loved me and that's all that I needed.

Anyone can do it if you believe it, have faith, and speak it into existence. Just remember it's not how you start, its how you finish and your latter will be greater. Trust in the Lord.

Through this book my goal is to help my Father win souls. We are taking back what the devil has taken from us. We are going to prove to Satan that we can do all things through Christ that strengthens us. I hope that you enjoy reading this book as I much as I enjoyed writing it. Be Blessed!

IN THE BEGINNING

God first started talking to me when I was a kid. Everything was so strange to me. I didn't know what was going on. In middle school, I battled with changing my life and giving it to Christ. I knew God said we could only serve one master, but I kept going back and forth. I knew where I wanted to be, but it was hard without a spiritual leader. I didn't have anyone to help me get through. My friends weren't into God at the time. Everyone was just so lost spiritually. When you don't have God in your life, you are lost and you get so caught up into Satan's diabolical ways.

Now, I'm so happy to say that I've found Christ and I am so content with my life. Whenever I face hard times my life continues to go on as if the problem isn't even there. This is how I know that God is with me and that there is change going on within me. Before I would panic and worry about tough times, but with God in my life, the tough times don't exist. I continue to believe, stay focus, and put my trust in God's hands.

When things are turned upside down and your way seems cloudy, it's hard to stay focused. I like to compare it to watching my favorite football team. Sometimes I still fumble the ball because I'm not focused. When you lose focus the devil comes right in and he steals your play and diverts your whole game. However, we all know that we are true believers in Christ and the game isn't over. Just because you're down doesn't mean that you are out. Now you are on the sideline coming up with a new strategy, except in your situation you are on your knees in prayer. You are praying that God brings you through the situation. When things appear to be awful, God can turn things around. You get the ball back in your corner and you run with it. One thing that we have to do is hold on to our faith, just as you are holding on to the ball. Think about this, you have the ball back in your favor and it's now your chance to lead your team into victory, but in actuality you're taking back your life from the devil. So you grab hold to the ball and run full speed ahead, never look back because that's how you lose focus and the devil gets in your head. You don't need to know how close behind you Satan is, all you need to do is make the touch down. God sent Jesus to be waiting for you at the end- your field goal. He is waiting on you to turn your life over to him. He's waiting with open arms to embrace you. Here's your chance. Only Jesus can save you. You are running full speed ahead and Touch Down!!!! You made it. The angels in the stadium are cheering you on. You made it!!! Can you feel that excitement? Do you feel the glory? Yes Lord, we did it. It's just that simple. Now Satan's game is ALL OVER. Jesus **saved** you. God didn't send you to fight the battle all by yourself. He gave his only begotten son and he also has angels camped all around you.

    I hope this message got through to you. It is very powerful. Sometimes you just have to look at things in different ways in order to get the message across. I know nothing about football as you can see, but God gave me that example to open the eyes of people. He put it in a way that everyone can understand. In this book, my testimonies are different from others; I used methods where everyone would be able to understand.

Where We Live

Kids are playing
And running in the street
Cars are rolling and switching beats

Cops patrolling
Trying to retrieve what's stolen

Drugs are sold
Like a story untold

Life's a disgrace
When you're living in this place

The Cosby's our show for after school
Theo and Cockroach trying to be cool

Education's important when you're in this social class
If you're not educated you'll finish last

As I continued to grow older there wasn't much change in my life, and it was especially hard not knowing God. I remember seeing spirits outside when I was just a kid. One Friday night I was looking out of the window at our front door. My parents were getting ready to go out and my other siblings were watching TGIF. I went to the door and stared outside and I saw a dog, a black dog with bloodshot red eyes. The dog stood in front of our steps and stared. I would close the curtain and peep back and forth, but that dog would never move. It was so strange to me and I was so afraid, but I never knew to just pray or to rebuke the devil from in front of our home. All I knew were myths when we were growing up of bad spirits and demons and things of that nature, but I really didn't know what was going on. All I could do in my youth was hope that there was another way to live life and hope that I could find it. I grew up living in fear. I saw kids dying at a young age and I was so afraid to die. I didn't know anything about Heaven or Hell. I just knew that I wanted my family to be together forever. I use to say that I was too young to die and one day my cousin told me that, "death didn't have an age, you can die when ever God comes for you." I didn't have a clue what she was talking about and ever since I was a little girl I was so afraid to die. I prayed every night that God would spare my life.

When I was in elementary school a child up the street died and I saw his body on the street. It happened just before we got out of school and the ambulance hadn't appeared on the sight yet. I was so afraid. One minute a child is here and the next minute their gone. My grandmother told me to pray. She told me every night when I said my prayers I should say, "The Lord is my shepherd and I shall not want." At that time I didn't know what that meant, but I felt safe. I felt protected by God and still today I still say those words. To me it helped me to fight the devil. I felt protected. My grandmother was shrewd and strong. I would always pray to be just like her. She had her flaws but she was a wonderful women. She was more than just my grandmother; she was my best friend and I love her with my entire heart R.I.P sister BeBe.

Another Way

In the ghetto
Or in the hood
I never quite just understood

Times are tough
When you're living it rough

No one's better
So we all stick together

I feel like I'm standing on a cliff
Staring and wondering "IF"

If I just jump and let go
My life would be no more

Maybe I'll just pray
And ask God to stay
Maybe He'll show me a better way

Life is confusing living in these parts
The devil is trying to get in your heart

He makes you feel so low
Then things are starting to move even slowly

Just reach out your hands and God will too
He's the kind of Man that will bring you through

UNDERSTANDING

    I've always believed in my poetry, it symbolizes my feelings and expresses my trials and tribulations. I strongly believe that God allowed me to use my poetry to testify about the obstacles that were placed in my life, and how he delivered me. My book is about how God gave me deliverance from the adversary. I want to use my deliverance, my healing, and my joy as a reflection to someone else's life. Read and understand what I went through and know and believe in your heart that God will bring you through. Always remember God is able and that he will never leave nor forsake you.

    In the beginning God made everything in this world, from the earth to you and me. Do you remember the song, "He's got the Whole World in His Hands"? Well God really does. One night I was getting ready to study the word of God and I was so excited. I was finishing Genesis and ready to move forward to Exodus. I said to myself, "I'm going to dedicate my next poem to Tarique Thompson." He's my friend's son and they are both very important to me. Then God lead me to writing Genesis. In the book of Genesis everything was created. At this point God knew the ending of the world and then came back and made the beginning. Think about this, God made victory in the end, and then he came back and gave us trials and tribulations to get to that victory. Nobody told us that the roads would be easy. There is a long road to victory, but it's worth the journey. When you're struggling and feel like giving up, think about the "Victory" that God promises us. In the process of reaching victory God also rewards us. There have been times when we wanted to give up, throw in the towel, or call it quits, but what if God gave up on us? He paid a major price for our sins. He died to save you and me and we want to give up. Do you know what He went through? We would never understand how one person could go through what Jesus has gone through for us. Do you know anyone who could be so mighty? Who could bear the pain that Jesus suffered? He was beaten, yet very brave to stand back up and struggled to carry His own cross to His place of Death? Jesus did this for us so that we could have life more and more abundantly. God sacrificed his only begotten son to die for our sin. How can we repay Him? We can repay Him by living righteous, living by His commandments, doing His will, being humble, and being obedient. Is that too much to ask for? Don't get me wrong, I fall short at times, but I don't give up and feel remorseful for myself. I continue to pray and allow God to help me put my life back on track.

Genesis

From the beauty of this nature
To the beauty of this land
Continue to believe God still has a plan

From the beauty of this Earth
To the growth of this nation
God has given us a new foundation

From the width of the seas
To the length of my hands
God has created a holy land

From the top of a mountain
To the bottom of the seas
God has provided for all of our needs

From the dust of the sand
Was the creation of a man
God has brought a person to the land

From the rib of this man
God united two hands
And that's how we got woman

From the beginning to the end
God created all men
And then he died for our Sin

HOLDING ON

When I was 10 years old, my father lost his job and my mother was the only one that was working. We lost our home that summer. It was a catastrophe. We lived in a minute 3-bedroom mobile home. I had 2 brothers and 2 sisters. It was hard growing up in a small community where nearly everyone lived in poverty. We had to share everything. My oldest sister and I lived with my Aunt and Uncle and the rest of my family lived at my grandmother's house with two other families. I stayed back and forth, mostly at my grandmother's to be with my younger sisters and brothers while my parents worked. It was so crowded, but God made a way. We have sacrificed and struggled our entire life, praying and waiting on God to give us a breakthrough. God brought us through the situation and I was so thankful. What I was most thankful about in that situation is that we had a roof over our head, food to eat, and clothes on our back. Most people wouldn't want to talk about the struggles that they had while growing up. I don't mind because it has shown me "Look where He brought me from" and I thank you Lord. My life is wonderful. I'm not rich, but my life is better and I used these hard times to help me to press on with my life. I'm grateful for the trials and tribulations. This is what brought me closer to God. God has been with me since birth. Even when we were going through this, I can recall God giving me a vision. He showed me that we would over come. He also revealed to me that he was going to bless us with another home, bigger than before, but most importantly it was going to be our home. He kept his promise; our new home was much bigger, we had more space, and it was a place that God gave us and that's what made it perfect. Losing our 1st home was the hardest thing. Everywhere we went people talked about us. Even our family would say negative remarks, but I expected that. When we went to school kids would ask when would we be getting a new home? The kids would be prying into our business. I'm past all of that now; I just wanted to share that my life was far from perfect. I went through the storm, but I survived. I'm so thankful that I went through things. When people come to me and talk about what they are going through, I can sympathize because I know how it feels to go through things. It made me who I am today. When people go through problems, I feel like I'm there. I'm able to go through it with them because God showed me the way; He has taught me how to have faith. In the beginning that sounds easy to do, but when your back is against the wall what can you do? I've learned my lesson and I can't preach this enough and you'll hear this throughout this book "God is able" and "He's a way maker." At times, it's hard to believe in something when you don't know where it's coming from, just have patience and always expect the unexpected.

Poverty

Twenty thousand a year
Man that ain't fair

Not enough space
We need a new place

Can't get government assistance
By $10 we just missed it

Driving a junk Cadillac
We just added a new rack

Wearing my neighbors hand me down
Now we're the talk of the town

Man, poverty has got me beat
My mother went to the market without shoes on her feet.

She rode my bike with a broken seat
Didn't have enough money to buy a pack of meat

That junk of a car has broken down
The tires are all over the ground

How do we fix this mess we live in
This is a sad story and I'm only ten.

MAKING SACRIFICES

    I started working when I was 14 years old to be able to provide for myself and to take the burden off of my parents. I was also helping my younger sisters and brothers. I had to have a sense of independence. While growing up I didn't have anything, but I appreciate every experience that I've encounter. I appreciate the obstacles I've faced is because it gives me power. It also allows me to get closer to God. The obstacles that I've faced have strengthened me and have given me a greater source of power. I've learned that power comes through the things that we suffer and the things that we sacrifice. When you think about it no one understands why we go through things in our lives. I read in "My Spiritual Inheritance," by Juanita Bynum that, "We have no power because we have no obedience." She also states, "We are not willing for our flesh to suffer in order to fulfill the fathers will." I've struggled and sacrifice throughout my life. I've come to the point where it doesn't bother me as much because I know God will make a way. When I was younger I didn't understand, but now as I've grown older I truly understand why we faced the storm.

    When I was growing up I spent a lot of time to myself. I felt like no one in my family liked me. I actually felt like a loner. I just wanted to be left alone. There were a lot of things that I was dealing with about myself. I would always have to baby-sit my younger sister and brothers and my dad would say to me for all of my hard work I would be rewarded. I didn't have a clue what he was talking about, but He continued to tell me that as I grew older. I thought he was just making that up. I was always expecting something right then. I would always look for it, but I never saw anything. I would just roll my eyes and be like whatever. Just recently, I realized that for all of the hard work that I put in, it was never in vain. Everything that you put your heart and soul into something good would come out of it. Back then my family was poor and my family wasn't able to give us incentives for the work that we did. As I grew older, my dad gave me everything that I ever ask for and the things that I didn't ask him for. When my job cut my pay my dad was the one that was making up the difference. When I decided to walk out on faith God blessed my dad where he was able to bless me. Even when my dad couldn't God has been making a way out of no way. God always came and delivered me right on time. There were times when I didn't have groceries or gas in my car to look for a job or to make it to an interview. God was by my side and He provided every step of the way. When people said to me, "How could you just quit your job? I really didn't feel like I owed them an explanation. All I could tell them is that I knew exactly what I was doing. I knew that my God was going to provide for me and I also knew that He was going to make a way. I believed that my journey wasn't going to be easy, but I was ready and willing to make the sacrifice.

    Sometimes in life we have to sacrifice and suffer to get what we really want. Don't ever be afraid. I use to worry because I was afraid that I wasn't good enough for God or I didn't know how I could learn all of the material. I also thought that I wouldn't be as good as the next person, but with time I've realized that I'm just as good as the next person. Never sell yourself short. I continued to seek God and asked Him to show me how to make things possible, to teach me like He taught Jesus, and to give me wisdom. I wanted to be prepared to fight this battle, just like David. Satan will attack, but I won't flee because I'm ready because my God has taught me.

Understanding

Why should you envy me
Is it because I have nothing?
Or is it because God blesses me with something

All of my life I felt like I had less
Now that I am blessed
I'm always trapped in someone's mess

I'm all give out till all I have left
Is to give myself
I try to share
But I'm all shared out

I can't keep giving
Because I wonder why I'm living
Every thing I got somebody wants to take it
I have one other question will I ever make it

I have no shirts
But I have a few pants
I have little education

But life still stands

I can't quit because then I'll be a failure
I can't start over because I'm turning like a fool
If I stop I might fall

I tried 180 degrees
But now I'm doing 360
Right back where I've always been
Nowhere

Life is really hard when you are trying to make it
Especially, when everything you got people try to take it

No one knows the way I feel
Hoping someday my heart will heal.

Days like this I'll never forget. No matter how far I've made it, I will never forget my past. In situations like these you learn to live from the experience and thrive off of it. However, you want to make sure that you are able to turn around and reach back and help someone else get out of their situation. It doesn't have to be financially, it can be words of encouragement. Do you know the story of Daniel in the Lion's Den? Daniel was thrown into a lion's den because he was caught praying to God. Daniel was faithful to God and he prayed three times that day, it was the day that all the governors had consulted together to establish a royal statutes and make a firm decree, that whoever petitions any god or man for thirty days, except the king, shall be cast into the den of lions. (Daniel 6) Daniel was in a very tough situation, but Daniel was a true believer and he knew that God would never leave nor forsake him. Do you think that God would leave his people? Daniel was praying to our Father and God came in and saved Daniel. He made it through the storm unharmed.

Think about a time when you were in the lion's Den at time when you were in a situation where you had to stay in prayer and wait on God to deliver you through the storm. This story leads me to write the poem called *Salvation*. As you read this poem just think about what I shared with you about Daniel in the Lion's Den.

I worked in retail selling shoes. A customer came in with a friend but she didn't have the money to buy the shoes that she wanted. She was very unhappy. I walked over and joined in on there conversation.

I told the customer that things will get better, just have patience. I continued to converse with the customers and I informed them about our layaway plan, which most customers are unaware of because employees do not promote it often. The friend then decided that she would place both pairs of shoes on layaway and suggested that they pay it off together. Also by putting two pairs of shoes on layaway they saved thirty dollars. When they got to the register they were very happy. I told the customer to look up to heaven and say, "Thank you Lord" because it was Him who made it possible. My manager and I were both standing at the register and when they were leaving she looked over to me and said I wasn't allowed to say the word Lord in the store, because it may offend people. I looked at her with disgust and then I commented, "Well let's see what God has to say about this tonight when I pray." She was very unhappy with the statement. I can't believe that people would actually stand for something like that; especially when God made everything possible for us. She of all people should understand, but not everyone is a true believer. I leave those people in God's hands. I know He'll take care of them.

Salvation

Whatever happens
I may say
It was meant to be
Just that way

I can't explain
The way I feel
Because my heart is wounded
And trying to heal

I'm trying to express my feelings inside
But I just can't figure out "Why"
I'm trying to be, so deep and smooth
But the room is spinning and I can't move

I'm trying to scream, "Help me" someone!
But I hear people laughing and making fun
Can someone hear me, making these sounds
Please don't make me go another round.

Can someone help me?
I need someone please!
Can someone be there?
To provide for my needs

I'm trapped in the basement
I don't have air

Help me please this is so unfair

Please let me out
I'm dying of drought
I need some water, just a drop in my mouth
I hear some footsteps coming down the stairs
I can feel someone, coming near
Lord I'm praying, to you in fear
Lord I can't stop crying, tear after tear

Wait

The door just opened and I can see someone
Is it you my father, the omnipotent one
Yes, it is you my lord, again I see
You gave your life to sacrifice for me

Thank you father for letting me free
Thank you father for saving me

PERSEVERING

When I graduated from high school, I wanted to go to Devry University in Decatur Ga., and my family could not afford it. My Dad was locked up, but he has always been a part of my life, and my mom couldn't afford to send me to school all by herself. One day on my way to work I was riding with my aunt and my cousin. I was lying on the back seat listening to some Gospel music. My aunt always played Gospel music and through the song, I heard someone speak my name. I couldn't believe it so I stopped to listen again. And the voice said to me, "Netta, you know what God wants you to do." I started to cry dramatically tear after tear. One, I knew God was delivering a message to me and two, because I didn't understand what was going on. That message was something that I could never forget. God has been speaking to me ever since. He has been revealing things to me and sometimes I still don't understand what is going on. At that time I felt I was being setback on my dream because we didn't have the money. Instead, I went to USC-Spartanburg, but had to start a semester late because there wasn't any housing available. In the meantime, I went to Horry-Georgetown Technical College and took a few classes until the next semester. This was still a great experience for me. I met a wonderful professor, Dr J. Hymes, who taught me a lot and I'm so thankful. I actually felt that I needed some improvement before I went off to a bigger University. I was so scared when that time came. I was 4 hours away from my family and I didn't have my driver's license or a car, so I was stuck in Spartanburg. It actually turned out to be really great. God has placed some wonderful people in my life that guided me and helped to bring out my full potential. Ms. Jones was my career advisor and she helped to mold me into the wonderful person that I am today. I was quite a mess, but she saw something in me and she brought it out of me. I worked hard for the change and it wasn't easy. I read this in Juanita Bynum's book My Spiritual Inheritance, "The way to ultimate power is through the direction of divine counsel. Sound spiritual counsel is our safety net. God's way always involves a process of coming through something in order to get to Him. Also, the Bible tells us we must be faithful in another man's work before God will give us our own." God has a plan for my life this I know, but He must see that I am ready to be a leader. Sometimes I become so nervous because I want to be able to do well and I want to make sure that my work pleases God. Lord, Father I pray that I meet your expectations. I just want you to be able to say to me, "My child, well done."

My Life

My life consist of me
Always unhappy

At times I'm spinning around
Because I have thoughts confound

I wish there was a way
That I could be happy one day

I try as hard as I can
But I'm turning like a fan

I wish I were a dove
Who soared around in love

I'm in search for more
But I need an opened door

I fail to understand that
I can't have this man

I appreciate what's given
And thank God for everyday that I'm living

If only you could see
How much a degree means to me

Only if though knew
Of what my life goes through

If only though could bear
Another second to spare

I'll tell you another story
About His mercies and glories

TRUSTING IN GOD

From my experiences God was doing something in my spirit, but I didn't know what was going on and I didn't have anyone who could be a spiritual leader so I had to figure things out on my own. When I was in the 11th grade my grandmother passed away and that following year, both of my grandfathers passed. My mothers' parents lived next door to us so we had the honor of growing up with my grandparents. Before my grandfather died, I saw my grandmother in a dream. We were all gathered at her house and there was a celebration going on. My grandmother was happy and dancing and then my aunt looked to her and said, "Mom you look so happy, but you do realize you are dead." My grandmother looked at her and her joy went away. She drifted away out of the door with a look of sorrow in her eyes. I then saw a clear white slipper and then some type of dirt, almost red clay. Shortly after that my grandfather died. I saw it coming, but I didn't know what was going on. I went to my aunt and she explained to me that my grandmother came back for my grandfather. However, I couldn't figure out why she came back in my dream. My grandmother and I were very close. She would be sitting on the porch when I came home from school and her house would be my first stop. I loved my grandmother. She would call me over to share a Pepsi or Coke with her. She loved Domino's pizza, but she didn't eat it all the time. I would help her rehearse for Easter. She would read a speech in church. She loved to look good. I think I got that from her. My grandmother always told me, "A women should be seen not heard." She taught me never to go out in the public and make a fool of myself and to never chase a man. My grandmother was very wise and she was always my best friend. I love you Sister BeBe. R.I.P

I CRIED

I cried because the sun didn't shine
I cried because he left me behind

I cried because of the changes of mood
I cried because I understood

I cried because no one was there
I cried because life seems so unfair

I cried because my daddy was gone
I cried because he left us all alone

I cried because I was hurt in wounds
I cried because I saw my grandmother in a tomb

I'm crying because I'm hurting inside
But I stand because I have pride

I cried dramatically tear after tear
I cried because I slept in fear

I cried because my best friend died
I cried because I'm trying to hide

I cried because I loved someone
I cried because his feelings were none

I'm thru with crying
I'm tired, I've tried
Now its time for me to find my happy side

I've cried so long till I'm all cried out
My life has to come out of this drought

My tears may come once in a while
But never in the same old style

God has been there to dry my tears
To comfort me because he cares

Crying is the last thing I'll do
I'll find a hobby, with something new

God will help you see things clear
He'll ease the pain and take away the fear

Just trust in him and understand
That he always have a master plan

God is so good to us when we are in doubt
He's the only one that could help us out

So call on God he's your only friend
He'll stand by you until the end

This poem symbolizes a lot of tragedy that happened to me while I was growing up. My dad went to jail my senior year in high school. It was right before my prom and weeks away from my high school graduation. It was so hurtful. There was so much pain that I had building up inside and I carried it for so long. My grandmother had passed away December 24, 1997 and both of my grandfathers passed away one week apart that following October. So yes, I was going through a rough time and then in 1999 my Dad went to jail. He served about 9 months for something as little as driving under suspension, but of course we all have a fiduciary to abide by the law. Then in 2001 my best friend died and that took an affect on me. One morning she was picking up her baby from the baby's fathers' house and I believe the story went like this, she was on her way back home and she ran off of the road and hit a tree; killing both her and the baby. She did leave behind a son who I love so much. I want to be a part of her son's life, but it is still so hard for me just because my best friend passed away. At this point I was just so wounded. At school my career advisor Ms. Jones recommended me to go to counseling. At first, I felt as if I had problems but was in denial, but after a while I accepted the offer and it actually did some good. I had a lot of knots tying in my stomach and if I didn't let go of some things, I could have hurt myself. God brought Ms. Jones into my life for several reasons, she wasn't just my career advisor; she is a spiritual leader as well. She knew what I was battling through and she stuck beside me because she knew God was in the making of something wonderful.

I am going to be honest with you; I was a mess, but look where he brought me from. I use to be apprehensive that I wouldn't be good enough for God, or that I was going to mess up, but look at me. I am honored to serve God. It is my pleasure. He is an amazing God and I am pleased that he chose me.

Throughout school, I have been thrown some curve balls. Some of them actually knocked me down. However, I didn't just lie there, I picked myself up and continued my journey. Everything wasn't always peachy, I went through some struggles, but I continued to trust in God and allow Him to make some drastic changes in my life. I'm not perfect, very far from it. I do still make mistakes, but I know that my God is forgiving. When I fall down, I pick myself up again. A professor of mine once said to me, "It doesn't matter how you begin, it's how you end that counts." Even with some of my classes, I started off struggling because I couldn't comprehend the material. I never gave up. I would always seek a source. I would turn to my teachers for help. Who knows the material better than they do? In life God is our teacher. When we can't do something or when we fail at something we can always turn to Him to help us get things back on track. Who knows how to get through things better than He does?

Glory

G- The G is for Glory because we magnify you
L- The L is for Lord, because we praise you
O- The O is for omnipotent, yes Lord you are the one
R- The R is for resurrection; you gave your only son
Y- The Y is for you Lord, because we magnify you, we praise you, and most of all we love you

"Glory Be to God"

INSIGHT

Before, I shared that my grandfather's death was only the beginning of my vision; I could see a lot of things. I just didn't know how to interpret what I was going through and I didn't have anyone to lead me to the right direction. When I saw my grandmother in a dream she looked beautiful like an angel. She was wearing a white gown. At the end of this particular dream my grandmother drifted away and all I could remember seeing was a pair of white shoes with some red dirt at the bottom. The next day, my aunt told me that my grandmother came back for someone and then my grandfather passed away. I guess my grandmother was happy, but she was also lonely. The two of them were attached. They spent a lot of time together. When I was in school, my grandparents would be sitting together on the porch waiting for the bus to come everyday. My grandparents were the ones who put me on the bus when I went to head start. I guess I actually spent a lot of time with them. It was probably because we lived next door to each other.

In undergrad I had friends that were going through things with their family and once two of my friends were experiencing death in their family. I didn't see them all week and I had a dream about what was going on, but they never told me anything. Later that week, I told them about my dream and they told me they were going home because someone in their family passed away and the funeral was that weekend. Do you think that this was just a coincidence or do you think that I was led by the spirit? I believe that God has given me a vision, but my next step is to figure out what am I suppose to do with it, as I'm led by the word everything will come in order. I do believe God is going to order my steps through His words. I'm so excited about this, I just hope that I do a good job and I live my life by God's words.

Continuing on with my vision, my senior year in college, my dad was working two jobs and my mom was working. They had a good income and my dad was paying for my car. I had a white Jeep Grand Cherokee. Well, things got a little tough and my dad was behind on my car payment and God showed me that times were going to get hard. He showed me that my car was going to be repossessed. I was so frantic; I would get up every morning and look out the door. I was so apprehensive. The devil was just taking control over my mind. I prayed everyday, but I was still afraid. God was giving me a heads up and preparing me for the storm. What I should have done was prayed and left it in God's hand and not be scared, but would that have changed anything? I should have rebuked the devil, but I fell right into his plans. The Devil is out to kill, steal, and destroy. My car was taken away. I was so hurt, sad and embarrassed. I cried for months. There was so much pain. At that time things were very hard. I couldn't afford to eat. I was in school and I didn't have any family around and no one I could turn to. At least no one I felt like I could confide in. I was terrified. I was so afraid. What was I going to do? I told my friends that my car was broken down and in the shop. I did have my best friend Kim and she helped me to get around. She was a true friend. She would get up early to give me a ride to school and made sure that everything in my life was okay. I cried so much because I grew up doing things for myself and I'm not the type of person who asked people for help. I just didn't know how to handle this all alone. I felt like the world had just turned its back on me. So I thought to myself what am I going to do? God showed me that people cared and that He would provide for me through this situation. I think that was the only way that I got through it. He brought really great people into my life. I met people in school who gave me a ride home daily. It wasn't bad, but it was painful. I don't know why because through a dream God had already showed me what was about to happen, but I didn't know how to act on it. He was preparing so that I would be aware. The night when I had to give my car up it was scornful. The guy who took it away was really nice. He came with his son and he knocked on my apt door. He told me that he would let me come and retrieve my belongings. He didn't have to do that but he did. From this incident, I realized that there are some really good people in the world who actually care about others. Satan tried to come against me, but I'm glad I knew God. I was stronger than I thought.

I'm a living witness that God is able. He said that He would never leave nor forsake us. When we go through situations, we should never think that God has left us. He'll walk through the storm with us, so He knows exactly what we are going through. He feels our pain. So wait on the Lord, be of good courage and He shall strengthen your heart but wait I said on the Lord. (Psalms 27:14) Just remember God is able. He's able to get you through any situation. In this particular situation He brought people in my life that volunteered to help me and as I continued to pray to God; He gave me the money to retrieve my car. The devil was so jealous because I turned to God and I put my trust in Him so he decided to sabotage God's work. When I redeemed my car, the transmission was gone because the car was towed the wrong way. My mother lost her job because she went to pick up my car and when she was on her way to Spartanburg from Statesboro, NC she could only drive 40 mph. She was late getting back home for work the next day and she was fired. The situation seemed as if it was getting worse. I just spent $1500.00 to get my car back, but God knew what Satan had planned and he stepped right in. One day I was walking across campus and I was talking to God asking him what to do next? How am I going to get my car fixed? I had my car towed to Leonard Bishop Transmission and he told me that it would cost $1000.00. Where was I going to get that kind of money? I only worked 30 hours a week and I could barely pay rent. God told me what to do and I went to the financial aid department and told them my situation. I was blessed with a grant that covered the cost of my car getting fixed and a little extra to help me make it through. Isn't God magnificent? He's been so good to me, better than these words can explain? He has given me direction, He's helped me to grow over the years, and He has taken my faith to a different level. For that I'm so grateful.

After I graduated from college, God continued to bless me. My car was beginning to disintegrate, so I prayed about it. I would be driving on 85 and I would see a Dodge Durango and I would say, "Lord that's my car" or I would just thank God because I knew that was going to be my new car and then God blessed me with that car. That was so amazing. I didn't plan on it or anything. I continued to thank Him and He gave me that car, which was a blessing from God. God said, "If you ask then you shall receive." Prayer is just as easy as it sounds; just keep remembering that God is able. He's our provider. He also knows your needs, wants, and the desires of your heart. There is power in obedience. You have to be willing to suffer in order to fulfill the will of God. You have to be willing to make some sacrifices. I look at things like this, in high school we had objectives that we had to master in order to move forward. If you didn't master them you had to continue retesting until you passed. In life the example is the same. God tests our faith, and when you don't master your test, you face those same problems over and over. I'll give you an example: I didn't make enough money to pay my rent and my car payment. I always had an eviction notice on my door. I'm not ashamed any more to talk about it. In the beginning, I was so afraid to be put on the street. I didn't know where I was going to go. My family told me to move back home, but I had to fulfill my dream, which was to graduate college. So I knew I had to deal with it. Then finally as it continued to happen, I wasn't afraid anymore. I just knew that I had to trust in God. I had to believe that He was going to make a way out of no way and that the situation was going to come to pass. It's not going to get any worse. Yes, to be honest it is hard when you don't know how the situation is going to change or when you don't know how you are going to take care of the matter, but God said that everything is going to come to pass. One thing that we must learn to do is learn the word of God, then be "Led by the Word," and know that the word is God. In Juanita Bynum's book, My Spiritual Inheritance she states that, "God's way always involves a process of coming through something in order to get to Him." It's true; just continue to read my testimonies. God brought me through these situations so that I could get closer to Him and also so that I would know whom He is and He wants us to know that He is God and God all by himself. Have you ever wondered what Pastor mean when they say that God wants us to become intimate with him? Well, God wants us to build a relationship with Him. God is so indescribable and He's so genuine. You have to build a relationship with him to know this. He's so omnipotent and there is no one in this world like him. My friend always told me that I'm so genuine. It's because my heart is wide open. When I was younger I would tell God that I wanted to be just like Him. He gave me a job to do and I won't let him down. Father I want everything that I do to be of your will.

God continued to speak to my spirit. Yet, I still didn't know where he was going with this; once God told me to walk away from my job, but I was so afraid. I didn't know how I was going to pay my bills, but that showed me that I had little faith in God. When I graduated from college I took a management position at the Waffle

House. I made $20,000 more from the previous year. The next year I made a $10,000 increase. So I was 24 years old and making $40,000. God is good and I couldn't complain, but I was so wrapped up into the money that I was making and when God was telling me to leave, I couldn't. The worst thing was I continued praying to God for a sign and when He gave it to me, I didn't want to listen. You can probably imagine what kind of punishment I received for being disobedient. God decreased my salary to show me that He was the source and the provider. He showed me that I can't do anything but through Him. He also showed me that he meant business; all I had to do was put my trust in Him and believe that He would never leave nor forsake me, and also I needed to be obedient to His words. I debated for a while just making sure that I was hearing God correctly. When I started listening to God I realized that in the beginning I wasn't obedient. When God told me to move I questioned him. When God speaks to us we have to listen, never ask what God has in store for you just follow his path and live righteous. In John 15:4-5, God said, "abide in me and I in you. As the branch cannot bear fruit of itself, unless it abides in the vines neither can you, unless you abide in me.

He also said, "I am the vine, you are the branches. He who abides in Me, and I in him, bears much fruits, for without Me you can do nothing. So with that said, All things are made possible through Christ who strengthens me. We can do NOTHING without God. Have **FAITH** in the **MASTER**, have **FAITH** in **GOD**.

One night while I was sleeping, I had my radio turned on because Gospel music comes on from 4am to 6am on 107.3 JAMZ. At this time God was still talking to me in my spirit and I was being submissive. I was listening to a song and through this song, I heard God directly telling me that I was created to make His name Glorious. That was pretty much the song that was on the radio, but

He was directing it to me and I was unsure about what He wanted me to do, but I know in due time He would guide my path. Another song that He spoke to me through was "Jesus would work it out." Every night my spirit would rejoice and dance when the song came on. I was shouting in my sleep. I could feel my body moving. I almost thought my soul was going to leap out of my body and shout. I've never felt anything like that before and I didn't know what to think, but I knew this was God working things out. So I was just getting ready because I knew he had something in store for me and I just knew I wanted to be ready.

These two songs, God used as symbolism. He was preparing me for my future. I needed to know that Jesus was going to work things out for me. It's amazing the way that God does things. I love this song so much because throughout my struggles I had to sacrifice and give up a lot, but as I continued to pray and magnify God, He gave everything back to me and he even rewarded me with things that I desired. I can truly say that I've been blessed. Although I was going through the storm, I didn't let that slow me down. I continued to do the will of God. The devil may have set some obstacles in my path, but I continued to praise God. It's amazing the way that God does things. I honestly believed that God wants me to magnify, glorify, and lift him up and that's what I intend to do.

Later on as I continued to listen, God began to speak to me more; and this time I was listening, and I moved when God told me to move. One night I was getting ready to go to bed and God told me that I was going to write some poetry and I said, "Lord, what will I write about?" and he said, "I'll give you the topics." So I wrote the topics down, which were: Dear God, Thank You God, and Glory. I told myself I would work on this tomorrow, but then God said, "NO! You will work on this now" and I said, "Yes Lord." So within moments I began to write and still today God put the words into my spirit and I write about things that happened in my life. Every poem that you read in this book I worked on because it symbolizes something that has happened in my life. I felt things and I acted upon them. Not only did God allow me to share my life story through my testimonies, He's used my poetry as my testimony also. My job is to promote God, to lift up his name, to praise Him, to magnify Him, and to teach his word in anyway that his people would understand. I'm so grateful to have this gift. I'm so grateful that God has chosen me. I'm so grateful that God used my experiences and me to reach out to you in ways that you would understand. It is my pleasure to be able to deliver God's words.

In John 15:6-7, God said, "If you abide in Me, and My words abide in you, you will ask what you desire, and it shall be done for you." Also He said, "If anyone not abide in Me, he is cast out as a branch and is withered; and they gather them and throw them into the fire and they burn."

Dear God

Dear God
I came here for a reason
It's the beginning of my new season
It's the ending of my old past.
I have a fresh start at last.

I put relationship and break up all behind me
But Satan keeps following, close behind me
I try to move on, because my new life has begun
But he insist on telling me this battle is won

I see a lot of strange things because the time is near
But I pray to my father, so I won't live in fear
The Devil is funny, he never gives up
My father is in heaven and to him I raise my cup

I raise a toast to you father, because soon we shall meet
At the gates of heaven, I reserved my seat
To all of my people who don't know what to do
Just call on my Father, he'll see you through

Thank You God

Thank you God for giving me the chance
Thank you God for holding my hands
Thank you God for showing me the way
Thank you God for letting me pray

Thank you God for making things clear
Thank you God for easing my fear
Without you God I would not know what to do
So thank you God for seeing me through

Thank you God, you mean the world to me
Without you Lord, who would I be?
It was you Lord, who taught me well
Yes, it was you Lord, I could tell

Thank you God for being my father
I thank you God because there is no other
Thank you God for being so true
Before I forget, Lord, there is none like you

The Conqueror

Who I am today
Won't be who I'll be tomorrow
We have to face the storm
In order to be transformed

You have to believe
In order to receive
Let the Holy-Ghost take you through
Exactly what God has in store for you

The storm will come and change day by day
Just look to heaven and begin to pray
Lord, my father, help me through the test
The day shall come where I could rest

These obstacles, I'm fighting seems stronger than me
I thank you father for changing who I be
I thank you father I'm counting my blessings
I'm grateful father I'm learning my lessons

These trials and tribulations are out of sight
I'm glad my spirit knows how to fight
This battle is won for you my Lord
I came here to fight with my sword

This pain I feel, Lord I can't not breathe
I'm trying to stay strong, I truly believe
I'm crying inside, I don't understand
I'm trying to keep my faith in your hands

Lord my father, I'm becoming weary each day
Please see me through this so I could stay
I'm here my father, here to do your plan
When it's all over, I could shout "Amen"

Saul

Saul lost every thing he had
Because he didn't listen
Now his blessing was taken and turned out missing

God gave him the orders
But he took the wrong path
Now he does see that misery does last

Next time Saul you'll learn to be humble
You messed up the play and made a fumble

You turned over your blessing
And gave it to David

Now David's the Prince
At your expense

Have you learned your lesson and taken God's blessing
Or will you be disobedient again and send your own message

Now crawl on your knees and beg God please
He'll forgive you and set your heart at ease

Cerrica

Cerrica was born in this world of Sin
Then Satan thought her life was going to end

Our families are here, we're praying together
So Cerrica's life can get better

The Devil created a disaster
But we all know whose our Master

So pray for Cerrica day by day
Because we want Cerrica's life to stay

Her sister is waiting for her to come home
Cerrica's a fighter and can make it through the storm

We love you Cerrica so don't give up
The Devil's a liar and will try to steal your victory cup

We know God has you in his hands
So Satan can take you out of his plans

We're counting on you to make it through
We're clapping and cheering, Cerrica we love you

GOD'S ANGEL

This poem is about a little girl whose life at the time was on the line because of a very diabolical situation that her parents placed her in; and that's just what the Devil wanted to see happen. However, this child is an Angel. God placed her here in this world, and we all know that God would never let anything happen to His anointing. One day, I was putting together this poem and I received a call and the caller told me that this child wasn't going to make it and that she had turned for the worst. God had just put this child into my spirit to pray, but he didn't say that anything was going to happen. So as I listened and my spirit told me that she was fine. Right then I knew that this child is a child of God and she's a fighter. She's been in the hospital since birth and has fought Chemotherapy. You can imagine what adults go through, but at that time she was an eight-month-old baby.

I began to pray, Father God in your name, the shameful and filthy hands that Satan has placed on this child's life, RELEASE it. Lord restore her strength as she continues to fight. Lord there is victory in this child because it took a lot for her to still be here. We thought she wasn't going to make it given the situation, but you saved her for a reason and for that Lord we Thank you. We thank you God just for showing Satan that prayer changes everything. This child is more than just a survivor, she's a conqueror through you Jesus, and she is now a living witness of you God and her life will be saved to praise your name. Lord I pray that there is Life in Cerrica, that there is Joy in Cerrica, that there is Prosperity in Cerrica, Lord and that there is obedience in Cerrica. I speak this in Jesus name. Amen.

A Dream Come True

She came in the world of sin
The devil thought her life was going to end

The family prayed together
So that we all can stay together

The devil created a disaster
But we know there is life ever after

So pray for this baby day by day
Because we want her life to stay

Her sister is waiting for her to come home
The baby's a fighter and can make it through the storm

We love you baby you're a child of God
This is your victory so take a bow.

Without You

Without you
I would be like a squirrel in a tree
Day to day running free

Without you I would be like a deer and a doe
Running wild with no where to go

Without you I'd be just like the season
Changing without any reason

Without you I'd be homeless somewhere
Staying on the streets and no one would care

Without you I'd be in prison
With thoughts of reasons for not living

Without you I'd be heart broken
With words unspoken

Without you I'd be as sick as a dog
Thinking that I didn't have very long

Without you I'd still be suffering and fighting
And waiting for someone to change the lighting

With You

With you I still have hopes and dreams
Finally understanding what things really mean

With you I have my degree
It's the thing that has set me free

With you I have my testimony
To give thanks to You, Lord only

With you I've learned to sacrifice
You told me to give up something twice

With you I've learned to stop and listen
I finally found the pieces that were missing

With you I've learn to hear your voice
Now I know how to make a choice

With you I've learned to connect too
I finally realize there is none like you

With you I've learned to stop and think
About the decisions that I make

With you I say, what would Jesus do
I know your heart is real and so true

Hey Little Cuz

Hey little cuz, you're only 15
Maybe it isn't, what it seems

Your life is just beginning
So look for a good ending
And you'll always be, the one who is winning

Acknowledge your work
And keep on striving
I'll commend your doings
As you keep on trying

Don't stay depress
And be so sad

Because the day will come cuz
When you'll be glad

Pray to God for your worries and pain
Because soon one day this world would come to an end

Just be patient and look above
The world is getting better and there will be much love

This poem is about a young girl searching in the world for love. She was lost and didn't have anyone to turn to, not even her mother. She had no direction. She grew up in a broken home with several sisters. All this you child ever wanted was a stable home for her and her sisters. Instead she had to work and take the responsibilities of a mother. Her mother was gone all of their lives. They grew up in an old unattended house and at times they didn't have food to eat. This was a hard situation for a child. Times were hard living in those parts. People just don't understand what little girls go through when they don't have either parent. They feel lost, unloved, sad, and will do anything to try and ease the pain away. No matter how hard you preach to them they still act out of anger and become lost in society. Although she didn't have her parents, if she would have found God she would have found the love that she was looking for. God has unconditional love that He gives us. He would never leave nor forsake her. He would have guided her into the right directions and have camped His angel all around her. He would have kept her safe from harm. She chose to fall in to Satan's diabolical path and now she's lost. The only thing that we can do for her now is PRAY. We all know that God is a way maker and that PRAYER changes everything.

    Let us pray, Father God in your name Jesus, I ask that you embrace this child and help her to realize what she's doing to herself and her family. Running away doesn't fix the problem. We need you Lord to save her because right now Lord, Satan has her wrapped around his hand and it is only you God that can change this situation. Lord Father there is none like you. Nobody can do it like you Jesus! Father we need Satan to know that this battle is yours; and that you have the victory. Satan uses the vulnerability of young people to draw them into his hands and then he corrupts them, but Lord we all know that not only will this bring her soul running back to you father, but also that there is always time to turn the situation around. Although this child is running, Lord she does know who you are and when she hears your voice she will come looking for you. You are so powerful Lord. When sheep's hear their shepherds' voice they will come running. Father God, allow her to embrace her situations and take her life back from Satan. Lord, I've tried my best to show her that she has choices Lord, but she chose her own path. Lord, all I know to do is to continue to pray because Prayer does changes everything. Lord, I thank you because I know change is here. It is here Lord because I can feel it.

A Chapter That's Closed

How could a chapter that's closed
Be easily exposed

How could something begin
If nothing has end

How could you try to move forward
When you keep looking backward

How could you say freedom at last
When you are holding on to your past

How could you ever be happy
If you are never sad

How could I earn your respect
When I do everything you expect

How could you expect a rainbow
If there is no rain

How could you expect diversity
If we were all just the same

How could we expect technology
If the world didn't change

How could we get strong
If the storm didn't come

How could we expect a breeze
If we didn't have trees

How could we expect respect
If we can't respect each other

How could we pick ourselves up
If we never stumble or fall

How could we succeed
Without a vision

How could we ask for forgiveness
When we can't forgive our neighbors

How could we get to the father
If we don't know his son

How could we get to the promise land
If we can't follow his path

And most of all

How could we make it to the gate
If we don't have any faith

DISCERNMENT

God has made everything possible for us. He has given us choices, examples and has shown us the way, but it is up to the individual to make the right decision. One thing that I want to teach to my family is that Jesus Is the Way, the Truth, and the Life. John 14:1-7 say, "Let not your heart be troubled; you believe in God, believe also in Me. In My Father's house are many mansions; if it were not so, I would have told you. I go to prepare a place for you."

"And if I go and prepare a place for you, I will come again and receive you to Myself; that where I am, there you may be also.

And where I go you know, and the way you know. I am the way, the truth, and the life. No one comes to the Father except through Me. If you had known Me, you would have known My Father also; and from now on you know Him and have seen Him."

It is imperative that we become intimate with Him. Understand what He has done for us. He sacrificed his only son to save our lives. What if our parents would have sacrificed one of us? How would we feel? What if we had to watch someone close to us beaten and there was nothing that we could do? We would feel hurt, we would probably be in rage, and we would never understand what was going on. We wouldn't know why this would be going on. We have to understand why God sacrificed Jesus. We need to know why Jesus died and how. We need to try and feel the pain that he went through. We need to know the path that He took, what's He's done to save his people, what's he's done to save you and me. We need to know God. We also need to know that God is coming back. Yes, He shall return and we must prepare ourselves so that we can go back with Him. When we leave this side we must be sure that there is a seat reserved with our name on it.

He Was Beaten

He suffered through the pain
When they tried to rip out his vain

He was terribly beaten
Through his crucifixion

He died for you and me
He gave us this world to see

He was a very strong man
Through his beaten He stand

He was sent by his father to save us from destruction
So we should follow his path, we don't need any instructions

His earthly mother watched and she cried
How petrifying it was to see her son beaten and then he died with pride

He wasn't here to stay
He was here to teach us God's way

He had to go home
To be with his father on the throne

He's coming back in the mist of the night
With power that is totally out of sight

He's coming back to this place
We'll finally meet him face to face

He's coming
He's coming

The time is almost near

He's coming
He's coming

So don't live in fear

Just live your life righteous and true
Just live by his words and you'll make it too

Let Us Pray-The Lord's Prayer

Our father who art in heaven, hallowed be thy name; thy kingdom come; thy will be done on earth as it is in heaven. Give us this day our daily bread. And forgive us our trespasses, as we forgive those who trespass against us. And lead us not into temptation, but deliver us from evil. For thine is the kingdom, and the power, and the glory forever. Amen

Because of You

It's because of you my dreams came true
It's because of you I can see things thru

I never thought I would see this day
I never thought I would feel this way

I never thought I would care so much
I won't ever forget you or your touch

I always thought you'd be by my side
I kept these feelings all inside

I miss you Boo and wonder why?
I've done all I could, I've even tried

Will We Stand a Chance

Will we always be ghetto
Or will we break out the habit of believing we will always be
black Negroes

Will we always be ignorant?
Or will we mature indignant

Because I'm black I show no pride
Or because I'm ignorant I try to hide

What I look for in this world is freedom and justice
But when we walk through the stores the white man don't trust us

In this world can I trust anybody?
I believe in myself and I know I'm somebody

Everything I have somebody wants to take it
There's just another question will I ever make it

This Joy I Have

This joy I have
I believe its love
I receive this joy from up above

It took some time
I'm happy it came
It's even helped me to glorify his name

This joy I have came in with the season
God gave me this joy for a good reason

This joy I have can't be taken away
I believe this joy is here to stay

So sit back joy, we're going for a ride
Or you can stay on the inside

This joy I have, I'm so grateful it's mine
I still believe my joy is a sign

That's okay I'm happy to be
With this joy of mine that's meant for me

I found this joy that I have once I surrendered and gave my life to Christ. No matter what I go through, nothing stops me from praising God. I'm learning to take on my problems and still continue to praise God. Before I felt so sad because God had given me everything that I could imagine and also the biggest smile that anyone could imagine. I quit my job in 2006. I continued to go to church and a special friend approached me and said to that she saw a glow. At that time, I'd heard it from several people. They said that they could hear it in my voice, see it in my face, and from that day I knew that it was deeply implanted in my soul that I was headed into the right direction. All I want to do is worship God, live righteous, be holy, and do right by God. This is my new passion. I feel so free. Free from all of the burdens that I faced working in that miserable place. Free from pretending to be happy in a very hostile environment. Free from crying at night because I was stressed out. The stress was taking over my body. Most importantly, my life and time was free and I am able to go to church. I am able to become closer with God and this was something that I prayed for many years. I can finally be fed the word of God and that, to me is, all the joy I need. I am so grateful that God has taken my life to another level. It has been a struggle, but I'm able to conquer anything. God has prepared me and I know that I can do all things through Jesus Christ who strengthens me. At first walking away didn't seem logical, but after I started going back to church I knew that was where I belonged. It was amazing, and well worth the sacrifice. I still have some ups and downs, but the one thing that I refuse to lose is this Joy that I have. It's magnificent.

New Life

This little boy is my son
I made him while just having fun

That doesn't mean life has to end
He's God's creation, life has just begun

There is new life in everything we do
Just make sure your prayer is true

He came into this world, He was sent by the Man
So rejoice and let this kid stand

God will show us what to do
When we sacrifice, he will take us through

So pray for this boy as he grows up
He's going to help us win the victory cup

My Gift

My Gift to you is Jesus Christ
He's the one who sacrifice

He's the one who built this land
He's the one who gave us man

He's the one who brought victory to me
He's the one who let me see

My biggest sacrifice to you
Is my father, who is so true

Thank you God for showing me the way
Thank you father for another day

Thank you God for being my gift
I am trying to give your name a lift

Be Who You Are

You can be as big as the moon
Or as bright as a star
But never forget to be who you are

You can lose your hopes
And forget your dreams
But life is never the way it seems

You can change your friends
Because friendship does end
But be sure the problem isn't within

You can run and hide
Or just tell lies
But the truth will come out from the inside

You can stay where you are
Or even move afar
But just never forget to be who you are

BE WHO YOU ARE

When I first started writing the poem, "Be Who You Are" I was thinking more about my brother and a situation he placed himself in. My brother wanted to live a fictitious life. He lived a life that he made up in his imagination and abruptly acted on and got caught into Satan's diabolical plans. Sometimes you see the life of other people and when you grow up lacking things it's hard. It's no excuse, but it's the life of many African American males growing up in poverty. It's a feeling of just wanting to fit in with others and you do anything to fulfill that dream. You get so drawn into the world, act out on your imagination, and don't realize what you are doing until everything comes to a halt. My brother made a mistake. He knows what he did was wrong and he admits to his mistakes. He's even apologized to the people that he has brought danger to. The thing that I don't understand is why do people put a label on others. When my brother was being sentenced, the judge felt he was a menace to society and needed maximum security. It was an attempted arm robbery and he never pulled out a weapon. He was more afraid than anything else trying to get away with a crime. If he was a menace he could have held someone hostage. The way he did the crime wasn't the crime of someone who actually wanted to hurt someone. There are so many people in this world who do things a lot worse and get off more easily. I'm upset because this happened to my brother and he is smarter than his actions, but I have faith and believe that God has mercy on him and he'll be released by the end of this year. My brother is a very smart individual. He was in college in Atlanta, Ga.

He was going through a hard time trying to make ends meet and came home for the summer and tried to find an easy way, but instead God spared him. He may not see it this way, but God saved his life. He could have been dead right now, but thank God, he's still alive to give his testimony. God has a plan and I know it's going to blow us away. I want to apologize for the harm that he may have caused others. If I felt that he was actually a threat to others, I wouldn't have written this. My brother and I are really close. I'm working with him to focus on Christ and understanding what he has done. I'm trying to show him how to be humble and obedient and to trust more in God in any situation. I believe that with prayer and obedience God will release him in 2008. I believe that he will be free this time next year. God is able and I know that he will find it in his heart to forgive my brother and give him a second chance. As long as my brother owns up to his mistake, which he has done, confess his sin, repents, and ask God for His forgiveness, and also learn his lesson then he'll be home for Christmas next year. I claim that in Jesus name. I expect the unexpected!

Undesirable

I can't stop this pain
My tear pours down like rain

I'm so down like a mother who just lost her child
I just want to run for many miles

What do I do Lord
What do I say
All I could do is kneel down and pray

How do I turn this around
How do I pick myself up off the ground

I'm so hurt, like a person who lost their best friend
I'm so hurt, like a person whose partners life just end

How do I get through this sorrow
This pain that I have is like no tomorrow

How do I get through this madness
How do I stop all this sadness

How do I keep moving on
When will this pain just be gone

Fools on the Run

I did it for love
I did it for me
I did it because I had to see

I tested your power
I ended up in sorrow
Now for us there is no tomorrow

We can run
But we can't hide

We can try to get away
But not very far

We can be like Harriet Tubman
Come on, I'll lead the way

Or how about Rosa Parks
The bus does get dark

We could be like Al Pacino
And try to blast away those fools

Or we can just surrender
And ask God to forgive us

A Tear of Happiness

A tear of happiness
A tear of joy
Why do people try to play me
Like I'm a toy
Whine me up or spin me around
Why can't my face change this frown

Why do I cry all night
Why do I put up little fight

Why do I live in such misery
When everything I have is given to me

Why do I pretend that nothings wrong
When I held these feelings for oh so long

Why do I hold all these feelings inside
And you look at me with such little pride

Why won't you just go away
There's really no need for you to stay

Cry no more
No more
No more

Those were the words given to me
Now I hope that you will just let me be

You have cause enough damage in my life
I feel like I've been stabbed with a knife

I'm sorry to approach you in this way
But you should find a child to play

I truly feel you should walk away
I'm a strong black women who knows her way

Look at all the damage you have cause
Leading women soul to be so lost

Maybe you should put in your mind, body, and soul
And watch how we leave you, oh so cold

Now you feel all the pain
Now give up brother your weak little game

Become a man and love me back
Or keep living your life so slack

Why can't you trust me just one time
Are you afraid to put your heart in mine

Keep on running and playing these games
When you try to love, it won't be the same

Don't come crying my feeling remains
When I wanted you badly you were so lame

Now she played you and your life is so thru
Don't come crying to me "Boo Whoo"

Now these pieces are coming together
I waited and waited, thought I'd love you forever

Maybe you're not the one for me
I prayed to God to let me see

Is this my true love waiting for me
Will this be the man that marries me

Will it be the man who hurted me so bad
The one I asked the Lord to give me his hand

I tried so hard to make this work
But is it really what its worth

I tried so hard, but it's taking so long
Sometimes I feel like my love is wrong

Good things come to those who wait
And to those who have greater faith

Friends

Friends are here to help you through
Just too bad there are only a few
Never give up and keep on trying
Even if in life you feel as if you were flying

Don't give up and aim high
Why are you running, we all are going to die
Sometimes life can get you really down
And friends are here to change your frown

Sometimes you make the wrong decision
I hate to see you end up in prison
I'm writing this because I'm your friend
And I hate to see your life just end

There's only one way to get on top
You can't start something and then just stop
I have problems that compares to yours
But guess what "God takes me through and open new doors"

I had a friend who was going through some tough situations. Ever since I knew him, people would take advantage of him. He did everything that he could to fit in and people mistreated him and that bothered me. To me, he never had any real friends. One day, he came to me at school and wanted to talk about some family problems. As I sat and listened to him, I could tell that he was wounded inside. He told me that he was thinking about dropping out of school. I knew it was the devil trying to set him back from focusing on his education. We talked a little longer before we had to return to class. When I got in class God placed these words in my heart and I wrote this poem to cheer him up. He told me that, no one had ever done anything nice like this for him and that he was very happy. We were really close. I was very happy too. I would always try to help anyone the best way that I could. Later on that day we were both riding with my cousin home from school and we stopped to the grocery store. My cousin and I were picking up groceries after school and my friend unfortunately got caught up. He found a purse that was dropped by an elderly lady on the floor. Instead of turning in the pocketbook he found, he took it and left out of the store. He was caught by the police and was arrested. It was so hurtful because I was just talking to him. Sometimes when people reach the bottom they do anything without thinking. They are just trying to find their way. I don't condone what he did, but I know that he is a good person who used bad judgment.

Trapped Between Love and States

Can love be confusing
Or are relationship amusing
Can I be in love
Or don't know what I'm thinking of

Do I just cross that path
Or do you just make me laugh
Why am I crazy over you?
Until I just don't know what to do

I should have let go, like you told me
Now I'm wishing that you were here just to hold me
I've been looking for love in all the wrong places
Then you came along and filled up the empty spaces

I don't want you to go, but we're in two different states
Being that I love you, I don't know want to make any mistakes
I just want to say, "I really love you"
And never the less, I'll be thinking of you

My Funny Valentine

If you stumble or fall
I'll catch you

When no one is there
I'll be there for you

If no one is watching
I'll watch after you

When times get hard
I'll be there for you

When you're far away
I'll always be with you

I'm running out of words
But I'll find a word for you

I'm just stalling time
To ask "Would you be
My Valentine"

The Color of My Skin

Because I'm black, should I be ashamed
Or because of my name, I get no fame

People cross me all the time
Trying to steal exactly what's mine

Struggling and trying, always depress
Can't wait for Spring Break just to rest

People around me look and they stare
I'm stared upon like a horror nightmare

Sometimes I feel like my friends are better than me
That's why I chill, to be who I be

I never worry about how I'm going to survive
I just study my work and try, try, try

I find myself thinking a lot
I'm trying to figure out what my life is all about

I know that I take things more than it seems
I just need to know exactly what things mean

I'm really focused on graduating from school
I'm trying to collect all data and tools

Once I went down the wrong path
If you try to change darkness won't last

I set some goals of things I want to accomplish
But people stand in my way and make me feel like I am nothing
Now all these years have passed me by
I'm aiming so high and trying to strive

I'm looking forward to December 2003
That the year I will receive my degree

The Death of Love

Why'd you do it
You killed my love
Watch it soar away like a dove

Away in the air
Watch the wings flare

All I wanted was love
But you couldn't do that
So I stayed in as long as I could
Probably longer than I should

I waited for you
While you loved someone else
I watched from the side
Thinking you were a special guy

Now that I'm gone don't worry with stress
Listen to these words
"I'll always love you," now please let me rest

LIFE'S STRUGGLES

Over the years, I've struggled with spiritual and worldly battles. Sometimes we pray that we find the right companion, but they don't always come when we want them to. I believe that Satan listens in on our prayer and as soon as he hears that we have some type of plan he puts stumbling blocks in our way. Every time I met a guy I would pray to God to give me a sign about this person and to reveal to me the things that I'm not seeing. I would say, "Lord let me know exactly what I was getting myself into and to show me things so I could protect myself." God revealed so much to me. I was just tired of being hurt to where I could never let my guard down. I started dating a guy and God showed me a lot of things about him. This particular guy is very special to me. It was so strange because he became my best friend. I was in the world and I wasn't living right at the time. I went through some ups and downs. I kept on praying. At this particular time he wasn't my boyfriend we were just good friends. We would talk on the phone all night until the next morning. Sometimes we would stay up all night watching movies. I knew so much about him and his family and he knew a lot about my family and me. We are still very close. At one point we had to take a break from each other because our lives were going in separate directions. Then I guess by the grace of God we regained our friendship. I remember one day he told me that things just fell back in place like normal. We had our trials and tribulations and our ups and downs, but I'm telling you prayer changes everything. I had some doubts about him, but when in doubt I kept on praying. He wasn't just someone who I fell in love with. I honestly believed God connected us for a reason. We were able to open up to each other. I always continue to pray because fighting Satan is an ongoing battle and he won't ease up for one second. I ask God to keep me protected and allow me to stay on top of things. Finding the right guy is a challenge, but let God lead you and stay in prayers. I was heart broken a lot, but I knew the right person would come along. Always remember to put God first. God will find that right person for you. Love is patient and kind; love is not jealous or boastful; it is not arrogant or rude. Love does not insist on its own way; it is not irritable or resentful; it does not rejoice at wrong but rejoices in the right. Love bears all things, believes all things, hopes all things, and endures all things. Love never ends; as for prophecies, they will pass away; as for tongues, they will cease; as for knowledge, it will pass away. 1 Corinthians 13:4-8

Goodbye Love Affair

My love was so sweet
It was more than just a treat

What is better than a sweet sensation
Wanting more than just relations

Wanting mind, body, and soul

Are you whole?

Trying to play me
Or trying to tease me

Which one?
Hope you had your fun

Can't stop thinking about you
Right now I don't know what I'm going to do

Will this love affair last forever
Or will we ever come together

No more cries
No more tears
No more time for love affairs

Being able to allow God to lead my life has been breathtaking. I've found myself in some tough situations, that I knew I couldn't get out of alone, but God was there. He has always been there to bring me through the storm and you have to understand that he can bring you through as well.

When you are facing a situation where you think that there is no way out or you feel as if you are facing a dark moment, always look up to heaven and seek the light. You can always call on God, no matter the minute or the hour, the time or the day, not even the season. God will always bring you through any situation, just have faith and trust and believe in him. Remember God is able and that God won't bring you to anything he can't bring you through.

Writing poetry is something that I enjoy doing because it allows me to express myself. At first I thought that my poetry was so elementary and that no one would want to read them, but then I realized that my poetry is so genuine and real. Some of my feelings came from what I've seen people go through, at times just talking with other people and realizing what they were facing at that time, and also from my own life's tragedy. I went through the storm and sometimes more than once because I didn't master it the first time. When I say I didn't master it the first time, I mean that I didn't get through it the way God intended for me to get through it. Let me elaborate so that you can fully understand.

When I was in high school, our classes had objectives that we had to master that were given by the school district in order for us to be able to move forward (State Requirements). If you didn't master the objective you would be retested until you were able to pass, but sometimes it would be a possibility that you could be held back if you didn't master the objective. In life the same rule applies. We go through trial and tribulations. God allows us to go through things to test our faith, but when we fail it is more than likely that test will come back around again. Sometimes we just stop and say, "Why is it that I'm always going through the same thing over and over?" Or we may even say, "I keep seeing the same thing," and then we ask God why. My explanation to this is you continue to go through this situation repeatedly because you haven't learned the lesson that God has set out for you. You should reevaluate your situation and try to figure out what was different the last time you went through it. Maybe you forgot to leave the problem in God's hands and that happens a lot. We give our problems to our father and ask him to take care of it, but then we take it back from Him and try to solve the problem ourselves. Let me give you another example, so that you can follow me.

One of my friends was headed in the wrong direction. She felt like she was in this world alone and no one loved her. She was facing problems since she was a kid. My friend really had a hard life growing up, but she could have used the hard times and the struggles as a reflection to move forward. She could have realized that she could have changed her situation, but she kept feeling sorry for herself. She hooked up with the wrong people and she took life for granted. There were alleged rumors that she was a prostitute and on drugs. It hurt me to my heart to believe that someone that I was so close to fell into the wrong path. I would pray to God daily, but I was still worrying. Every time I would get the chance, I would go and see her and try to speak words of encouragement, but it didn't work. I thought I could fix the problem. I wanted to fix the problem so badly, but that situation was in God's hands. I was in school so I was trying to keep updates on her and see what was going on. I was so mad and disturbed. I had so much rage built up inside of me because I couldn't get through to her. Later I had a one on one talk with God and I finally surrendered all of the pain, worrying, and suffering that I was putting myself through into his hands. The night I broke down and finally left all of my problems in Gods was the best thing that I could have done for her and myself. That night I felt something happening to me. I prayed to God and he lifted the burden straight off of me. I confessed with my tongue that I couldn't handle that situation and that the battle belonged to Him. I apologized for giving Him the problem and taking it back. I finally realized that I couldn't fix it. I was deliberately tearing myself apart. Sometimes we wish that we could protect the ones we love and we would do all that we could trying, but in actuality God is the only one who can save our lives from destruction. She's still out there wandering around lost, but I continue to pray that God would deliver her from her mistakes and sins. I want to pray that God protects her and that she leaves the world of darkness and come into the light. I pray that she allows God to save her before it is too late. No matter how bad the situation may appear to be, God can fix it and He will. We have to believe.

    In the poem I wrote, *The Conqueror*, no matter who you are today won't be who you are tomorrow. You have to know and realize that people change. The word conquer is defined as, to overcome, to defeat, to take control of, to get the better of, triumph. No matter what kind of turmoil that Satan plans to set into your path, overcome the situation, or make plans to defeat the devil. However, you must be prepared for a fight. Don't think for one second that Satan is going to walk away, he is very consistent, but with the proper nourishment and I mean being fed the word you can give Satan his

Final Disconnection. Imagine God sending over an Angel to Satan; and the Angel hands over a piece of paper, a letter, that says "You Have Been served." Now Satan has his final disconnection. He has no more control over anyone's life. His powers are demolished. All of his plans have failed and he has no more use to anyone. Goodbye Satan you are through. God's won this battle and not you.

Satan's Final Disconnection

This is your final disconnection
God has given us resurrection
He gave His only son
A new life has just begun

No more fun and games
It's time to praise God's name
I'm walking away from my past
I have joy at last

The sun is Oh! So bright
God has given me greater height
God has given me power and authority
He's put my testimony in my poetry

He's given me time to realize
How you just like to demoralize
So give up Satan you are through
God's won this battle, not you

One thing that I've learned about Satan is when he's aware that he can't destroy you in one area he will find an area that you are struggling in to try and bring you down. After I stopped worrying about my financial situation, how I was going to pay my bills, how I was going to be able to save money all over again, or the anxiety of looking for a new job he noticed that those areas in my life were covered and I had joy. Even though I didn't have money I still had joy and the devil couldn't take that away, this Joy I have is for me. Everywhere I went people told me that they saw a glow. Satan couldn't reach me in that area so he found a new area to focus on. He tried to come into my relationship with my companion, but again that didn't work. I knew that my relationship had room for improvement, so I continued to pray that God would help to build us on a sturdy foundation. I knew that there was going to be ups and downs, but I refuse to let the diabolical Satan attack my family or friends. I stay in the word to keep us protected. If he finds the smallest crack in your wall he sees that as an entrance. So my word to you is to fill all cracks and holes. When there is any sign of instability in your relationship with family or friends, Satan will be out to ruin you. So my words to you are to stay in prayers. It is the only way you will be protected.

No matter what your weaknesses are Satan will use those weaknesses as an area to attack you. He will scandalize your name, demoralize you, and get as low as trying to get into your thoughts and make you feel like you are nothing, but it is you that has to be able to know how malevolent Satan is and that he is out to kill, steal, and destroy. Don't think for one second that he is your friend. God said that he will never leave nor forsake you. God promises to give you the needs, wants, and the desire of your heart. He also promises us eternal life. Satan can't give you any of that, only a one-way ticket to Hell. That is why it is imperative that we find God and we hold on to Him and the love that He gives us.

I know sometimes we face problems that may appear to be so appalling and we wonder why God allows us to go through something like that especially after we've asked Him to take care of us. That could be one reason why people are afraid to put all of their trust in Him because they don't get the results that they are looking for or sometimes people feel like they need a break and God wouldn't give them one.

You have to realize that we go through tough situations so that we can become closer to God. He wants us to call on his name. He wants to be our protector. He wants to become intimate with us. He wants us to know who He is and in order for US to do that you have to get to know Him.

I remember when I first got my drivers license and my first car. It was a 1995, white, Jeep Cherokee. I just loved that car. I called it kee-kee. I was so afraid to drive. Every time I got into my car I would pray that I would be safe and that God would protect me from all harm. I was a nervous wreck. Everywhere I went I would have my brother drive me. I was so scared because I had just learned to drive that summer before school started back and it was in a small town not to far from Myrtle Beach, but I went to school in a bigger city further away from where I lived. So there was a big difference. One day, I was on my way to class and it was my brother, my friend, and myself and I was at the stop sign at the head of our apartment complex. I drove to far up and I was going to back up a little, I looked behind me, but I didn't see the car behind me and I backed into the person behind me. Thank God there weren't any damages and he was nice about the situation. I was so afraid. I was so mad at God because I expected him to protect me. I felt like he didn't own up to his words. Later that night, I was coming from my friend's house and when I was turning on my road I went over the speed bump and everything just blacked out and things started looking kind of fuzzy. When I was driving into the spot I was to close to my neighbor's car and when I was going to back out, my wheel was turned and I scraped the side of his car with mine. I was lucky that there weren't any real damages done to any of the cars. The guy understood and said that he was okay about it. I was so hurt, I felt like a complete failure. My brother helped me repair the damages made to my truck so that my parents wouldn't see it. Later on that night I was praying to God. I was in a complete frenzy. I was so upset when I asked God to protect me. I was mad with him for a few days, but then once I calmed down and realize whom I was upset with I realized what Satan was trying to do to me. First of all he used the fear that I had to turn me against God. I just wanted to be safe from harm. What I didn't realize is that God didn't leave me nor forsake me.

    The situation could have escalated into something a lot worse, but through it all he spared my life, but I didn't see that. All I knew was that he had let me down. And that's exactly what Satan wanted me to believe. Satan wanted me to believe that My Father had turned his back on me. Now God turned the situation around and helped me to get through my fear. I apologized to him because I was looking at things in the wrong way. God has always been so good to me. He's always brought me through every situation. I have an intimate relationship with God and it's because of the obstacles that I had to go through. So I'm actually thankful for every experience that I've encountered. Satan thought that he was putting a blockage in my path, but what he has done for me is helped me to get closer to My Father. That means that Satan still ended up a loser in that situation also. You have to remember Satan is going to try and play all of his cards, but it is up to you to see right through him.

I made the biggest sacrifice of my life in 2006. I quit a job that gave me financial stability. It wasn't just an ordinary job; it came with struggles. I felt like I was backed into a corner and I couldn't breathe. It was actually causing my health to fail. I was so stressed out that I got an ulcer. I kept praying about the situation, but when God gave me an answer I wasn't listening. He told me to walk away and that He would take care of me. I just didn't know how I was going to make it. I was afraid that I was going to lose everything again. I just didn't want to go through the pain, heartache, and humiliation. So I continued to work there, but I was punished because I wasn't obedient. The money that I chose over God, He took it all away. I was making 700 less a month, but I continued to see things my way and tried to make things work. I would cry to my dad every day and he told me that I needed to step out on faith and that God would provide for me. I should have listened to my dad and My Father, but I kept on pushing. I knew God is able and my dad was going through a similar situation and he stepped out and God provided for him abundantly. God was so good to him to where my dad was able to bless me and that's' how I was able to make it. I know that God would make a way out of no way.

Do you remember when Jesus fed 5000 people with two fish and five loaves of bread (St. Matthew 14:17)? Or when Jesus told Peter to go and catch a fish, and in the mouth of that fish was enough money to pay the taxes they owed? I am a living witness of the miracles that God provides. When I left my job on a medical leave I didn't have any money coming in and I was raising my nephew. God gave us food to eat and paid my bills. At first I didn't know what was going to happen. It was so hard and I was afraid. I would call my mother daily and cry because I didn't know how I was going to make it. My mother would tell me to pray about it. I was so irate because I was sacrificing for myself and now I had an innocent child that I had to sacrifice for also. I couldn't turn my back on him because he was going to start school in the fall and I didn't want him to go back into the world. Also I mentioned it is our job to reach back and help someone else. When I went to college I had a lot of support from my aunts and uncles. So many people were praying for me. I don't care what anyone says prayer does change everything. Sometimes we get all worked up and try to change people's situations. I've learned that job belongs to God. The only thing we can do for a person is pray for them because that is the only way you can save their life. God is the only one who can deliver a person, so put it in His hands and leave it there.

• Another miracle was when Jesus spoke to the winds and the waves in the storm and said peace be still. (St. Mark 4:39).
• The fourth was when Jesus walked on the water. (St. Mark 6:48)
• The fifth miracle was when he was casting out demons.
    (St. Matthew 8:16)
• The sixth miracle was opening the blind men's eyes.
    (St. Mark 8:23-25)
• The seventh miracle that came before him so vividly was healing of the women who touched the hem of his garment. (St. Mark 5:25-29)

  All of those miracles may seem impossible, but we know that God is almighty. He's the maker of the Heaven and the Earth and he has control over our lives. God gave up everything to give us life. He made the biggest sacrifice ever and what could we offer him that could ever compare? All God ask is that we humble ourselves, Be earnest in him, have holiness in our prayers, be obedient, and live by his commandments.

> For God so loved the world that he gave his
> Only Son, that whoever believes in him
> Should not perish but have eternal life.
> For God sent the Son into the world, not to
> Condemn the world, but that the world
> Might be saved through him. He who believes in
> Him is not condemned; He who does not believe in him
> is condemned already because He has not believed in the name
> of the only Son of God. (John 3:16-18)

The point I'm trying to make is that God is able to do all things. I can't preach this enough. A few days ago I went to the state Prison to visit my brother. He committed arm robbery the night of his 21st birthday. He was turning 21 on July 7th 2004 and he went to jail a little after mid-night. This had a big impact on my family. My brother was attending college in Atlanta, Ga. He is a very smart individual that just made some poor choices. No matter what he has done, I still think that he's wonderful. He's my brother and I love him. My family looked down on him. They talked behind our backs, scandalized his name, but we paid them no mind. We left this in God's hand because everyone makes mistakes and only God is in charge on Judgment Day. The only thing that I want to say about this situation is that God forgives us for our wrong doings. Jesus can save us from destruction. Sin doesn't have a value; and no sin is greater than the other. My brother always wanted to keep up with the Jones' but we didn't have it like that. We grew up in 3- bedroom mobile home in Georgetown, SC. My parents worked to provide for our needs, but we lived in poverty. When we were growing up it didn't seem that way because everyone around us was in the same situation, but once we started growing older it finally became noticeable. We all started working at a young age. I started working at an early age. It was horrible but it helped me to buy what I needed. I'm grateful that I had the opportunity. It made me who I am today, strong and independent. Anyway, my brother looked at entertainers as idols and he wanted that life style, but he went about it the wrong way. He wanted to be a "baller," he wanted to be noticed, and not just some broke kid who came from a poor family. He had big dreams, but got caught up in satanic ways and that easy when you're not saved, sanctified, and filled with the Holy Ghost.

It is so easy for young people to live the fast life and not think about the contingency of what could happen when it's all over. If God didn't step in when He did, Lord knows what else could have happened. If you think about this his friend Satan led him astray. Now people may look at this situation as something negative, but I'm going to bring out the good in the situation. You have a kid who's confused and has God on one hand and Satan on the other. He's being pulled on both sides. He chose the diabolical because it looked good, it sounded good, but we all know that there is no good in Satan. So our God, who is a jealous God, stepped back, but he knew that young man would be back. He knew that Satan is no one's friend. He knew what Satan had planned. So of course, he got caught red handed. Sin was written all over him. So now he's going to jail. What happened to your friend? You had no friend remember, Satan doesn't care about you. Satan can't make any promises. Only God will be by your side no matter how many times you turn your back on him. He's a forgiving God. Do you know of any parents that would turn their back on their flesh and blood? God loves us no matter what. He'll always be there with open arms. "Come back to ME," he says. So now he's in jail and he's asking God for forgiveness and he's confessing his sins and God is listening. When his trial came up he got 10 years in prison, but this is not the end of things. Now he has to realize that God's been there all the time. He just has some down time to reflect back on life. God is going to change his situation. He just has to seek God. God is a way maker. He will make a way out of nowhere and I'm a living witness. My brother didn't want to wait on God to change his situation when he was growing up. He wanted things to fast and didn't want to wait on God, but here is his testing time. He was so eager to do things the wrong way. Now he has to do what? "Wait on God." This is one process that he can't speed up. God is on God's time. My brother wouldn't be in this situation if he would just be patient and go through the trials that God set for him so that his faith in God could be tested. Even while he's in prison, he's still going through the same trial. Sometimes we don't always have money to send him. He understands that we have rough times also, but not long ago, God pointed something out to me. When I went to visit my brother, I had to sit down and talk to him because he was missing a very valuable lesson. I explained to him what he was doing all over again and that was not trusting in God. He wanted things now and he couldn't wait on God. I said to him, you are facing the same trial again; you need to sacrifice and trust in God. Psalms 27:14 says, Wait on the Lord: Be of good courage, And he shall strengthen your heart; Wait, I say, on the Lord. I'm so glad that I caught that because he was about to fail again. Sometimes we miss what God is taking us through. If I didn't catch him he would have probably missed it again. We have to go through the storm in order to be transformed. We have to let God take us through exactly what he has in store for us. Remember *The Conqueror*- just refer back to the poem. See my brother was doing it again. He wasn't getting what he needed and he became impatient. Whenever we didn't have the money to give him he would ask other family members to help him and when they weren't able he would feel let down. God didn't intend for anyone to bless him. It isn't this season. He has to wait.

God put that in my spirit. I'm so glad that the Lord is using me to be an influence on my family. I'm more of a Leader. The spirit of the Lord has taught me a whole lot over the years. On the downside, when my brother was indicted, it took a toll on my family. We had so much anger and animosity built up toward others that we failed to realize that God had his own agenda and that he was working things out. My brother could have been dead. The police could have shot him just because he was a black male. He was arrested in Horry County and Myrtle Beach is very racist. So God saved him from destruction. He could have hurt someone and really the law did what they were supposed to. Let's remember that God had to protect the other people that were in the restaurant. They had to feel safe. I think that my brother is learning his lesson and I pray that God will over come this situation and allow him a second chance at freedom. My brother has committed a crime, but I don't feel as if he is a threat to society. He was just a kid who took the wrong path. He just needed some positive people in life that could show him how to work hard and have all of the wonderful things in life. He needed to work on having patience. He also needed to know that God would provide for the wants, needs, and desires of our hearts. My mother went to church, but the foundation wasn't sturdy enough. I'm so glad that I branched off and found some magnificent people who has guided my life and shared some of their experiences with me. I'm also grateful that God has given me the opportunity to become intimate with him and to face my own obstacles. I must admit that I've had some good days and some sleepless night, but everything that I've ever been through was for a reason. I am now able to understand things from a different perspective

When I was a young girl, I use to go to church but I really didn't understand what was going on. At that time I didn't realize the role that God played in our lives. I remembered Rev. Bonnie Green use to sing this song in church "He made a way" by the time she got to "God made a way for me"; She would be shouting all over the place. Rev. Bonnie's song stood out to me the most because at that time. I had no clue what she was talking about. Now as I think back on Rev. Green and why that song touched her most. I can truly say, "I understand why she sung that song every Sunday in church." God is a way maker. He's been making a way for me, a way out of nowhere. I remember times when I couldn't pay my rent. Every month I had a notice on my door. God has been so good to where he would allow my land lord to change the lock's on my door and I would spend the night with my friends and when I got my rent money, I was able to pay it and then move back into my apartment. My Landlord wasn't just an ordinary Landlord she was a women of God who would always tell me to go home and pray. She understood everything that I was going through. She could have turned her back on me but she didn't she knew that God was going to be there right on time. She understood and I'm so grateful that she helped me get through that. I could have been homeless, but it was GOD, Who made a way. God made it where everywhere that I went his people would be camped around me. He nurtured and embraced me with open arms while I went through this world trying to make a way. I'm telling you people wake up and count your blessings. We can't make it without

God. We can't do these things all on our own and we can't fight these battles without a wise leader, one who would sacrifice His life for yours and still help you to make it to victory. That's the kind of God I serve and you could too. Now Satan, he wants you to follow him, but when things get bad will he risk his life for yours, will he show you the way to salvation? He will leave you in the mist of your tears, he's not your friend; he's the enemy.

A while back, I was working for a company that in the beginning was so great. I had a vision when I first started working there. I learned a lot from management. However, I won't ever forget how corrupt that company is and how people just cover up their wrong doings. I wonder how companies manage to stay on top when they are unethical and dishonest. I worked so hard for this company. I worked very long hours and I took verbal abuse. There were people who actually tried to dictate my life. Sometimes they felt like they were helping, but they just felt the need to just pry. Once I was hurt on the job and I felt like things were going to take a turn, I was right. Everything went downhill. I worked for this company for a long time and I sacrificed some things, but nothing was good enough for them. I felt like I was chased out. I suffered an ulcer for over a year from all of the stress that I went through working there. I went to the doctor every week. I had drug users working in my restaurant, thieves, and lots of drama. I
had to get away from that place. I dealt with racist remarks from the employees, and customers. When I finally decided to walk away from that organization they tried to put a halt on my life. They kept calling me daily to come back to work just to cover their tracks, knowing that they did a lot of unjust or they allowed it to go on. I just wanted to walk away and move on with my life. Instead, I had to continue to recap the reason that I left my last employer every time I went on an interview. Even when I tried to file for unemployment,

I caught a hard time. Even though my situation was so messed up working there the unemployment commission decided in their favor. My question was how someone could tell me when I had a good enough reason to leave my job. I felt like I was retaliated upon because of my work injury and I took legal procedures. When I needed help management turned their back on me. When I received the letter from the administrator-hearing officer, I cried for an hour. I couldn't believe that they actually wanted me to go back in there after all I went through. They said that the employer gave me several options and I turned them down and I didn't give them time to rectify the situation. How many chances did I need to give them? I gave them plenty of chance to fix lots of situations, but they always did what was best for them to make money and not what was best for me. I had to deal with racist remarks from the public and the employees. I had to deal with 2 dishonest bosses that lied, cheat, and stole from me. I felt like I was working directly for Satan. I was the one going through these situations and finally I decided that was enough. I was so upset when I got turned down for unemployment. In addition, I had an ulcer from the stress, two injuries and surgery all in the same year, but they wanted me to continue to work.

This particular day, I was turned down for two job positions and coming home to find more bad news, which devastated me even more. I wept and then I asked God to "please have mercy on me" and to help me." I felt like my world was over and I began to lose hope. I was going through it and I couldn't figure out why. I wanted to give up but God told me to pick up my bible and turn to John 13:7, It reads, "What I am doing you do not understand now, but you will know after this." With those words, my heart was at ease.

A week ago before all of this, I was warned of the hard times that were coming. I even dreamt of me crying out to God to have mercy. I began to think, if everything has came to pass the storm should be coming to an end. I think in this situation, I was afraid that I was going to lose everything like before. It's not easy when you feel like you are in a similar situation. I just didn't want to go through all of that pain and embarrassment again. I knew that God wouldn't put me through anything He couldn't bring me through. He is a way maker and He is able. These situations would only make me stronger.

At this time, I reached a dry patch in my life. I ran out of resources and I didn't know what to do. I kept on praying, but I was always looking for the results right then and I knew that God didn't operate like that. He's an on time God, and He'll be there right on time. At this point I didn't know what I was going through. Every bill that I had was now overdue. I kept praying but I got nothing, no result. I just kept telling the bill collectors that I would be in there as soon as I could, but that didn't stop them from calling. I was at the point where the bill collectors were threatening me to take back everything. I wasn't afraid, but as I continued to get closer to the deadline I got nervous. I just couldn't see anything. Everything was so cloudy and I didn't have any options, but to call on God. I went to my friend to borrow the money and she said she could help me. The day before she was supposed to give me the money, she had an unexpected bill that she needed to pay. Then I asked my mom to help me and she said to me that she had to take care of some bills that she had. I told her that it was okay. A few days later my mom said that she would give me the money and I told her that I didn't want to accept the money. After I asked my mom the first time and she said she couldn't; it was then that I realized that I needed to "Wait on the Lord and be of good courage, And He would strengthen my heart, so I waited on the Lord.

No matter how many ways that I tried to prepare for myself they all failed. It was time to give it all to Jesus, and not worry about it. Not every one is able to see something like that. When I told the lender who financed my car this story she said to me at this point one payment wouldn't be accepted. I would need two. I told her that God blessed me with this car and I don't see him taking it away. So we just have to see what happens. God wouldn't allow me to lose everything again. My back was against the wall but I knew that he was going to save me. I am like the little boy in my poem Salvation. If I continue to wait, my savior would rescue me. I knew my Father was on the way. I was heading into the same direction as my brother by not trusting in God, but I caught it. I didn't have patience to get through the storm. I was trying to get through it alone and its' hard.

I kept wondering, Lord why am I going through this. Everything seemed so familiar. It reminded me of when I was in undergrad and I didn't have enough finances to make it. Well I believe the first time when I went through this God went through it with me, but this time He was watching over me as I master this objective.

It's just like when a person teaches a child to ride a bike. In the beginning you hold on to them to protect them, to teach them, to coach them through it, and to nurture them. Once you get the understanding of it you are watched over from the sideline and to make sure that everything is okay.

I believe that God is testing me. I know He has something remarkable in store for me and He wants to make sure that I'm strong enough to handle my task. It takes a lot for a person to see what is going on in their on life. I always prayed to God that he would use me to do something special. I continue to pray daily that His will be done.

I was facing the storm, but I came out with my hands up shouting victory, God has been opening doors for me. It's been amazing. I'm so glad that I was able to go through this and still be able to stay focused. God is a good God. I struggled in the beginning, but as he continued to equip me, I became ready to battle.

One day I was on my way to a job interview and I was thinking about how people always rely on other people's experiences to take risks or to make their own opinion about something. An example would be when people want to use a new product they always ask others for advice. If someone wants to go skydiving they would ask the advice of someone else before they do it. Now trials and tribulations are something that we all face and most people get through their problems by confiding in others who's been through a similar situation. It gives them hope that they will be able to conquer their situation. So I believe that this book is an inspirational reference that people can read and refer to when they go through spiritual battles. They can use my life's stories and my trials and tribulations as an image of how hard life could be and how to get through those obstacles. This book is a true story of everything that I've been through. I'm preparing you for the storm. I'm giving you the nourishment that you need to get through the storm. We all know that storms can be bad especially when you're living your life for Christ. If we don't prepare ourselves through God's words and without the proper nourishment we won't be able to conquer. When we're in school our professors or teachers gives us all the data and tools that we need to become educated in certain areas and to pass our test. God gave us teachers that He chose to deliver his words. So it's the same as being in school. God gave us resources and we have to use them. We have to utilize our resources because it they are there to help us. I just hope that "Led by the Word" is a great help to you and that this book touches many lives. God allowed me to do this for a reason. I'm here to help spread his words and be a living witness of who He is and His work. I'm grateful that I'm able to reach out to someone else who's going through something. It was really challenging, but if you follow my walk with God you will see some amazing things that He has done in my life. I've found my joy and I found it through Christ. I now know who I am and I know my purpose. I hope that you've enjoyed the beginning of my journey. God Bless!

ABOUT THE AUTHOR

Twanja Windley is a Black African American female who is transforming her life to do the will of God. She grew up in a minute community called Plantersville in Georgetown SC. She graduated from Choppee High School. She received a degree in Business Administration at the University of SC in Spartanburg, SC. She received an MBA with emphasis in Human Recourses Management from Webster University. She's a member at Redemption World Outreach Church in Greenville, SC.

She grew up in a large family filled with love. God has delivered her through lots of circumstances and that's what led her to writing this book. It was the will of God. She first started writing poetry when she was younger spending time at the Mall with her cousin Edrica. She used poetry to minister her feelings.

As the years went by, she was out of work on a medical leave, and as she spent time with God, He began to minster to her again and she began writing. God spoke to her in the spirit and told her that she was going to write some poetry and then she began her journey. In the beginning she was just going to make a book of poems, but then she was led by the word to allow her poetry to be a part of her testimonies. God has blessed her abundantly and she wants to bless others by ministering the words of God to youths, teenagers, and adults. She wants to help take someone else's life to another level. She believes that God has put into her spirit to magnify His name, to lift up His name, to glorify Him, and to deliver His words and that's the vision that she sets out to do. This work of God "Led by the

Word" will take your life to a different level. God gives us different references to help us to get where we need to be and she hopes this one works out perfectly for you.

Use her life as a reflection. See beyond your current situation and focus more on the future. There is victory ahead if you only keep your eyes on the prize. Remember the storm won't last always, why because God has given us His promise. He promised that He would not flood the earth again. That means the storm has to end.

Printed in the United States
145989LV00001B/114/P